A Guide
For
Associate Ministers

A Guide For Associate Ministers

A convenient reference

for

associates in ministry

By Reginald D. Terry

A Guide for Associate Ministers

(A Convenient Reference for Associates in Ministry)
Scripture quotations from KJV

Copyright © 1999 by Reginald D. Terry

ISBN 0-910683-47-6

To the memory of my father,
Reverend Alvin William Terry (1933-1992)
and other fallen pastors
who served with great distinction
and without notoriety, yet selflessly tutored
countless associate ministers
to make them better servants
for the Lord Jesus Christ.

Contents

Preface

This publication stems from a conversation I had with one of my associate ministers. In a private conference we discussed various aspects of the ministry, which included my making some specific observations concerning approaches to preaching and the recent sermons he had preached before our congregation. There the Lord overwhelmed me with a tremendous burden that there was no manual or handbook (that I was aware of) to address the redundant issues pastors face when ministering to associate ministers. How many times have pastors exchanged ideas about how to deal with situations involving associate ministers? How many times have pastors had to re-cover topics for new associate ministers that the pastor has heard, experienced, witnessed and learned, yet have never seen in print? The inspiration was quite clear. The only thing to do was to face the challenge of this arduous assignment and discipline myself to take the necessary time to compile the information contained herein.

Many of these practices are considered universally acceptable among Baptists; however, one would not find them necessarily included in a manual on ministerial ethics or polity. The need for a text that proposes some uniform guidelines for encouraging and instructing associate ministers in their service to pastors was the impetus for this work.

The author in no wise attempts to convey that he is a final authority on these matters. This effort is merely a compilation of the thoughts and opinions of numerous pastors and ministers who have found themselves without the benefit of a written script to which they could refer. It is my earnest hope and prayer that God would be glorified, that all ministers would be edified, and that the people of God would certainly be blessed by what has been assembled. I now offer a simple and basic guide that speaks quite plainly and particularly to the issues and idiosyncrasies inherent to the role of the associate minister. Many already agree that considering the magnitude of this subject matter, a hand-book of this kind is long overdue.

Acknowledgments

I simply do not possess the capacity to list the names of the countless men and women that help to inform my positions and perspectives as I engage ministry. I was born in a home where the man who gave leadership to our development was both our father and pastor, so his efforts to serve the cause of Christ really provided my first seminary classroom experience. I thank God for the privilege of being nurtured in and growing up under the influence of my dad, the late Rev. A. William Terry. His reprimands and rhetoric continue to shape my thinking even years beyond his final falling asleep. God's name forever be praised.

In that same environment was the loving attendance of my mother and his partner for life, Mrs. Romanetha R. Terry. Her quiet walk with the Lord still blesses the small community where we grew up. Together they prepared myself, Llewellyn Eugene and John Fitzgerald (both preachers of the Gospel), and our sweet sister, Angela Yvonne. Considering the many people in community whose immediate families are unsaved, it is a comforting joy to know that our parents determined to personally introduce to each of us the Lord Jesus Christ. If we never get to see each other again on "this side," their parenting ministry has guaranteed us a family reunion on "the other side" that cannot be surpassed. Hallelujah, to the Lamb!

My thanks are also extended to my beloved Antioch Baptist Church in Omaha, Nebraska, whose pulpit and study have afforded me a platform to further develop my endowments as a pastor, preacher, practitioner, and person. Without their patience and understanding (especially during our initial days), no doubt this publication would never have been written.

A final expression of thanks to my two associate ministers whose zeal for ministry sparked the fire that caused this writing to emerge. May they find strength and encouragement from these pages as we partner together to do the work of our Lord.

Introduction

The people of God were worn and weary. Like a band of wandering nomads, they drifted from place to place as the Lord commanded them. In the intense heat of the Desert of Sin, they found rest at Rephidim, yet they were not refreshed. What a tragic dilemma it is to be able to rest, but not be refreshed. The problem was that there was no water for the Israelite community to drink. With lips parched from the noonday sun, their frustration turned into complaining. In their minds, death was certain and their only recourse was to blast the one person who was responsible for their predicament. They raised the indicting question, "Is the Lord with us or not?" (Exodus 17:7). Realizing the likely repercussions from their complaint, Moses cries out to the Lord for relief, and God answered his prayer (see Exodus 17).

Not long after that crisis, a new crisis developed. Some fierce enemies of God's people staged an all-out attack on them while the Israelites quenched their thirst at Rephidim. Isn't that just like life? "If it ain't one thing, it's another." Right before the water incident at Horeb, they were complaining about the menu to Moses. It seems that their deliverance from bondage did not deliver them from their memories of Egypt. They remembered the meaty meals while slaves, and the delightful diets of depression. Freedom was fine, but not if they could not have food. One can only imagine how the Lord's servant might have felt. God came through again.

Now here come the Amalekites. And they weren't playing either. The Devil never plays with the people of God. Warfare

1

is serious business. Moses, though barely able to catch his breath from the last two crises, was now facing another tense situation. From within the membership, he selects a brother named Joshua to lead the forces into battle against the enemy. The weight of all of this chaos is surely taking its toll on Moses. Nearing one hundred years old, he takes his position atop a mountain (like a general standing over his troops on the battlefield) with his staff in his hands raised high before the people. Exhausted from the conditions in the plains and the complaints of the people, the arms of the mighty man of God grow weary. The battle is taking more time than could have been anticipated. He reasserts himself and raises the staff high again, clearly worn from the encouraging task at hand. It is encouraging because as long as Moses' arms were up, the Israelites were winning. When his arms grew tired and were lowered, the Amakelites prevailed.

Observant to this action were two alert members (they were actually young ministers) of the congregation named Aaron and Hur. I can imagine they watched him for a while, feeling his pain and fatigue. I can see them in my mind watching him, and intermittently looking at each other as his arms would rise and fall, rise and fall. After a final glance at each other, they simultaneously move towards his aching side. Sensitive to the weakening man of God, and the mission that the membership was trying to accomplish, these associates assume a support posture to simply hold up the pastor's arms until sunset (when the battle was over). What a marvelous picture—to see some other members of the team, not trying to discredit or damage their tiring leader, but rather offering themselves to help him in an area where he desperately needed and wanted their assistance. In effect, this pair literally became partners with the pastor in the accomplishment of their common mission. That is what every one of God's leaders needs—some willing workers, some sensitive supporters, some partners with the pastor, some able assistants who are committed to ministering to, rather than menacing their leader.

The story in Exodus 17 perfectly models for us what associate ministers can do and be for a pastor. Aaron and Hur volunteered to intervene during a critical situation that had communal implications. Had they remained in the "pew" (or comfortable in their seats on the rostrum), the effects of their neglect would have been disastrous beyond estimation. These two ministers were quietly and cooperatively working alongside the servant of the Lord, encouraging the work of ministry for the benefit of the "church."

Of all the books written for pastors and ministers, I have never seen a manual designed to encourage the role that every pastor entered before ever realizing a call to a church. Before we were ever called Pastor or extended an invitation to serve the needs of a congregation as its leader, before our names were ever painted on a marquis, each of us were associate ministers in a church. We were associates in the sense that we did exactly that: we associated (or affiliated) with that particular ministry. Without a specific title, with no particular assignment, nor even an area of ministry responsibility, our first charge was simply to be good understudies, watching, working, waiting, but most of all willing to do whatever we were asked to do by our pastor.

This handy reference book is to humbly offer some hints from our history to assist the new minister and the more mature associates as they assume this assignment to be "on the team" with the pastor in the accomplishment of God's mission. Whatever else you may do, make sure you are at least guilty of holding up the pastor's arms.

The Call to Ministry

God calls ministers. The Old and New Testaments are replete with instances where individuals heard the clarion call of God, inviting them into His service to perform some particular task in accordance with His will (see Jeremiah 1). This divine encounter generally is an invitation to persons who unquestionably have a heart for God, a love for God's people, and have demonstrated a specific burden towards the selfless commitment to encourage their salvation. As a general rule, a call to ministry (Christian service) is ordinarily preceded by a call to salvation. All too often, persons experience some uniquely strange or possibly life-threatening ordeal, and assume that God is thereby summonsing them into the Gospel ministry. Many times, God is simply allowing those situations to occur in order to call one from "...darkness into His marvelous light" (1 Peter 2:9).

In this consideration, babies are never seen managing the checkbook and handling adult responsibilities in the home. The life of Moses is a perfect example of this truth. Biblical history reveals that after forty years of living in Egypt on the conveniences of Pharaoh's control, Moses spent the next forty years of his life in the Midian desert with a priest for a mentor (Exodus 3:1). Before Moses' ministry began as deliverer and lawgiver, God allowed him to be spiritually tutored by a man (Jethro) who just happened to be his father-in-law. Likewise, the new convert should be careful to learn as much about God and get as close to Him as possible before becoming too anxious about telling mature believers what to do and how to live.

The call is not a call to "be seen" or to "sit" in a particular seat in the sanctuary. It is absolutely and unequivocally a call to service. It requires true Christian devotion, a commitment to "go" whenever and wherever the Lord should direct, and a willingness to be held absolutely accountable by one's minister and church family. Such devotion was apparent in the life of Elisha the son Shaphat, when Elijah came to Damacscus (1 Kings 19: 16-21). Elisha's service to Elijah went from going everywhere that Elijah went to pouring water on Elijah's hands. He clearly understood that his role in the relationship was simply to make sure that the Lord's chosen vessel was properly attended to, and that his needs were met.

While Elisha was clearly anointed to become Elijah's successor (see 1 Kings 19:16), he had no problem in his "support" role, waiting on the servant of the Lord "hand and foot." This type of service requires an extreme amount of patience and humility. One needs patience because of the nature of the assignment (having to wait on another person who serves in leadership over us). Humility is needed because when you, too, have been anointed, you have to be careful not to consider it beneath you or that you are "too big" to play a secondary role in the interest of kingdom service. Our first responsibility is undoubtedly to God. This is definitely His ministry and we are in His employ. Nonetheless, if a person is unwilling to be a genuine servant, and is unable to be totally honest and completely open with his or her mentor and spiritual confidant (ideally this would be one's pastor), then that person, in my estimation, is not ready to respond to the call to preach.

The actual call of God is a uniquely different spiritual encounter. Throughout the Scriptures, God has in peculiar ways revealed Himself to His people. For Moses, the Lord drew him to the far side of Mount Sinai in the Midian desert, and spoke to him from within a burning bush (Exodus 3:1ff). For the boy Samuel, it was while resting in the temple in the employ of the priest Eli that he heard a nocturnal Voice calling him by name (1 Samuel 3:2). Elijah heard the voice of God while retreating under a juniper tree near a ravine, east of the Jordan (1 Kings 17:2). The prophet Isaiah reflected on his own call experience in the year that King Uzziah died, and described that memorable event in decisive detail (Isaiah 6:1).

Even in the New Testament, the Lord continued to enlist human participation in His redemptive work. Peter was invited to do His bidding while fishing on the Sea of Galilee (Matthew 4:18). The beloved Apostle Paul was dramatically drafted into our Lord's service while traveling the Damascus Road (Acts 9:1-9). Each of these calls was distinctly different, yet they were all a clear invitation to become involved in the peculiar work of God that we know as ministry.

One should notice that none of these persons sought the ministry as a professional vocation or a career. Their involvement in this important work is a clear response of surrender to God's specific will and purpose for their lives. Too many individuals have entered this sacred work without a good understanding of this reality. Subsequently, their service lacks commitment and the people of God (even the ministry itself) suffer incalculably. This lack of a knowledgeable perspective about the call to ministry has caused some to become involved in this challenging labor just to "get paid" or to have a public forum for promoting themselves or their personal agendas. This type of "hustling" mentality has literally crippled the credibility of preachers and ministers to a diastrous degree. Whenever a call is sensed, a person should immediately seek the prayerful intervention and loving support of their family, their pastor or minister, and perhaps the confidential intercession of one other person whose walk with God is clearly recognized and highly respected.

Areas of Service

Every minister is not necessarily called to be a pastor. Effective ministry is not limited to the arena of the traditional church setting. There are many other legitimate areas of service to which God calls individuals. It is most unfortunate that our preaching tradition has left the wrongful impression that the only fulfilling forum wherein ones can exercise their gifts is in parish ministry. Even pastors have been guilty of perpetuating this misconception by sadly regarding non-pastors with an air of contempt. Church staff ministry is a viable and validating area to which one might be called (i.e., Minister of Christian Education, Minister of Youth, Minister of Counseling, etc.), and never sense a desire to become a pastor. One can be very fulfilled and quite content in these and several other areas of ministry.

For instance, the ministry of full-time evangelism is one area in particular to which few (in our culture) devote their total energies. Most evangelists who lead revivals in churches around the country have congregations that they serve as well. Paul clearly emphasized to the believers at Ephesus that "… he gave *some* apostles; and *some* prophets; and *some* evangelists; and *some* pastors and teachers…" (Ephesians 4:11, italics mine). This is a critical area of Christian service that many should prayerfully consider when seeking to discover in which area the Lord is leading them to work.

The teaching ministry is another area wherein one can obtain a sense of legitimate usefulness as they serve the cause of Christ. This area of sacrifice can be either in a local church or in the realm of academia (higher education). Even beyond these, creating and offering community Bible study group encounters helps one to discover and cultivate their specific gifts and interests while serving the Master. Institutional chaplaincy offers a tremendous challenge for persons whose inclinations are not to serve in the traditional church setting (i.e., service to the military, hospital ministry, and prison ministry). Although the majority of relationships in these settings are transient, the quality of service offered does not have to be compromised for the benefit of the people. God does work in and through chaplains who effectively encourage the hearts and minds of His people who are a part of institutional communities.

There yet remain numerous other opportunities for persons to minister to the legitimate needs of hurting human beings—substance abuse ministry, homeless ministry, geriatrics ministry (nursing homes and seniors' complexes), the mission field, ministry in the corporate sector for the high stress of big business, and many more. With a heart to genuinely serve the Lord, one could easily find a sense of personal value in a number of areas of ministry other than inside the local church.

Perhaps this is one of the reasons why a call to ministry is usually accompanied by a subsequent opportunity to share an initial sermon before the congregation where one's membership is recognized. While the call is indeed personal, it is deeply rooted and realized in community. The church (a baptized body of believers) is afforded the bona fide responsibility of authenticating (confirming) the minister's claim to have been commissioned by the Lord to engage in this specific area of Christian work. This responsibility should be assumed sacredly and seriously. Too many congregations have regretfully endorsed persons for the preaching ministry who have not demonstrated a clear propensity towards the preaching craft. This miscalculation is often due to the sad confusion experienced simply because a person has the ability to sing with passion and feeling. Other times it is due to a family or congregation that wishfully encourages individuals into ministry (much like peer pressure among teens) because of the assumed prestige of the position or because another family member is involved in ministry. For many such persons, perhaps their calling could be to become involved in some other area of ministry service for the cause of Christ.

Licensing

The general practice among Baptists is that a license is granted to such persons who, believing that they have been called, have undeniably demonstrated a spiritual inclination to proclaim the Gospel. Whenever a license is given, it is only a certificate of endorsement (or approval) by the church that the so named individual has their blessings to pursue this course, and may upon receiving an invitation, exercise such gift to the glory of God. It is literally a certificate of permission or approval, and not authority. While the license is most times given to the new minister, it should be understood that the document is actually the property of the church. Ideally, it should be maintained on file and in the control of the church until such time that the associate is either ordained for a specific assignment or otherwise moving to a new location (perhaps out of town). Some advocate that the license should be mailed to the licentiate's new church family for maintaining until a call has been extended which requires ordination. These and other careful management practices encourage accountability to help ensure that the preaching ministry is not taken lightly. The license simply infers that the congregation has corroborated the claim by the person, that God has indeed endowed that individual with the ability to communicate His message to His people with a reasonable degree of competence and effectiveness. It goes without saying that an observable deep commitment to godly living is fundamental in this equation.

With rare exception, churches will readily confer licenses upon individuals who suggest that they have been called to preach. This matter should be considered carefully by every church so charged with this task, because everybody who musters up enough courage to stand before a congregation of believers should not necessarily be afforded a license to preach. Some should be admonished to go to school, or maybe to consider a different area of service, or perhaps afforded (at best) an opportunity to try it again (if warranted). Teaching a Sunday school class or Bible study group could aid the prospective minister in speaking before a group, and also enhancing the discipline of preparation. Leading a specific area of ministry (a youth group, an outreach team, or some evangelism witnesses) may distinguish an individual's commitment to the call. Much prayer should be given to this assignment.

Suggested Steps for Licensing

1. The person(s) sensing God's call to Christian ministry should with much prayer immediately confer with their pastor for counsel and direction.
2. The pastor (if not already doing so) should begin prayerfully regarding that individual's life, witness, and commitment to the church (i.e., attendance at worships, prayer meetings, Bible study and other activities, and also to see if the prospect is demonstrating good stewardship practices).
3. The pastor should schedule several sessions with this person to discuss various aspects of the actual call experience to confirm what God may (or may not) be saying.
4. If warranted, the pastor may inform the diaconate (the deacons and deaconesses), and possibly the congregation of the person's inclination towards the preaching ministry, and enlist their specific prayers for God's blessings and confirmation regarding the same.
5. Once reasonably convinced, the pastor should publicly offer a personal belief statement concerning the person

under consideration, and recommend to the church that the individual be afforded an opportunity to deliver an initial (trial) sermon.

6. The church should approve the pastor's recommendation.
7. A mutually agreed upon date and time should be set for the hearing of the initial message with announcements and notices being relayed to the church and the community. This sermon does not have to happen on Sunday.

It should be clearly understood that an initial sermonic presentation is not an automatic guarantee that one will be granted a license, whether the sermon verified or disclaimed the assertions of the individual. A period of time may need to lapse, during which the individual can be given future opportunities to share messages until such time that a comfortable degree of competence is obtained.

Ordination

Ordination (or being set apart) is the rite of passage that signifies that a person has been called or commissioned to a specialized area of ministry by a fellowship of believers. Specific gifts and certain qualifications help to justify such decisions by a church or a pastor. Ordination should not be sought or desired in the interest of simply securing a church pastorate. In gist, there is no need for ordination if there is no specific role or position that requires such. At the appropriate time, a church may take the necessary steps to either request or have a minister ordained, should an opportunity to serve them in a specific role be extended. Ordination is granted as a result of the community of faith having recognized (1) an individual's calling for ministry, (2) a demonstrated commitment to preaching, and (3) the capability of handling specific responsibilities associated with the work of the pastorate.

Suggested Steps in Preparing for Ordination

1. The candidate should be a licensed minister of the Gospel from a properly recognized Baptist church.
2. Ordination should always be preceded by a specific (official) call to the candidate to serve in a capacity wherein the responsibilities of that church, agency, institution, or organization stipulate a need for such. A letter requesting ordination may be initiated by either of these entities.
3. Upon written verification of the same, the pastor of the candidate should present a recommendation to the church requesting this action.
4. The ordaining church should endorse and approve this recommendation.
5. At the pastor's direction and initiative the ordaining church will extend invitations to assemble a council of pastors (other ordained ministers) charged with the responsibility of examining the candidate (either privately or publicly) to determine the prospect's proficiency for the impending assignment.
6. The council should meet (in advance of the investigation) to organize and prepare for the formal inquisition.

A Suggested Process for Ordination

1. On the appointed date and time of ordination, the pastor may introduce or present the candidate by name, along with some biographical information, family association, educational background, and any other relevant matters germane to the candidate's Christian experience.
2. The candidate may be given an opportunity to offer a brief opening statement indicating his or her gratitude to the council for their apparent sacrifice, and perhaps a minor elaboration on any personal history that might be relevant.
3. A written credo statement (a position paper on one's

beliefs) should already be prepared and copied by the candidate for distribution to each member of the council. It should address the candidate's personal conversion, a description of the specific call experience, a basic understanding of Baptist church doctrine and polity, and the ministry of the pastorate. This will also give the Council an idea of the candidate's style and written communication ability.

4. The catechizer (or the council, if permitted) should raise other relevant questions that concentrate on the following areas: (1) Personal, (2) Doctrinal, (3) Ecclesiastical, (4) Community, and perhaps, (5) Contemporary Issues. It must be understood that the purpose of these questions is not to embarrass or unduly harass the candidate. It is simply to ascertain proficiency in these critical areas of Baptist church life. No controversial questions should be allowed by anyone on the council, and especially none to which the asker has no qualified answer.

There does not appear to be a uniform set of questions that are used to examine a candidate during ordination. Various approaches have been employed to engage this labor. While this text does respect the sacred rite of autonomy for pastors and churches, a list of common questions is provided in the appendix of this book to offer some form of unanimity for this assignment for the benefit of both pastors and preachers who may soon be part of the ordination process.

Training and Education

It is my firm position that a call to preach is nothing less than a call to preparation. This reality has been tragically ignored by many who simply want to have it known that they are a "preacher." Doctors are not permitted to practice medicine without having successfully completed a specified course of study, and further passing the American Medical Association's qualifying examination. Lawyers are not permitted to practice law without having finished their course work and subsequently passing their bar examination. Teachers in the classroom cannot instruct our children without having obtained their degree, and then passing a teacher's examination. If such is the case with physicians, attorneys, and teachers, surely the church should take a more serious look at the basic requirements for training related to ones whose callings affect the most critical part of the human existence, the soul.

With contemporary congregations becoming more academically astute, and the modern pew being indubitably more biblically literate than at any other time in human history, it is essential that ministers take the necessary measures to become better qualified educationally to offer the best quality service to a congregation and community. Such training is not limited to accredited seminaries and Bible colleges alone (though whenever possible these are highly encouraged). Most local communities are periodically favored with preaching seminars, workshops and clinics, or training opportunities to encourage and further equip ministers who are interested to take advantage of such events. Scholarships, grants, and other assistance are sufficiently available for those seriously interested in improving their endowments in God's employ. If one simply wants to, God is certainly able to open doors and create ways for these coveted privileges to become possible.

Many argue the position that "I don't need to go to school," in light of the spiritual distinction of our calling. "Can't no man tell me what to do about God's business," some have suggested. These are certainly weak arguments at best. Indeed ours is a spiritual pursuit; however, it must be understood that education is an integral part of it. One desperately needs formal training. The classroom setting

offers a controlled environment for spiritual reflection and
healthy exchange with other practitioners who are facing
similar, if not the same dilemmas. It enhances one's study
habits, shapes one's ministry practices, and encourages disciplined thinking for a life of dedicated service. The elders
have said through the years, "you may get your 'burning'
(referring to the inspired call from God), but you also need
some 'learning!'" There is clearly no excuse for ignorance
in ministry as we strive for optimum effectiveness in the
new millenium. Dr. Fred G. Sampson, of the Tabernacle
Church in Detroit, Michigan, has often said, "There is nothing wrong with being dumb, but it's stupid to stay that way."

Consider for a moment the fact that healing is a spiritual
gift. What if every physician took the position that they did
not need education since God gave them the gift of healing?
Few of us, if any, would be standing in line for appointments
with them during a need for some specialized surgical procedure. Even beyond the classroom and years after one's
seminary experience, the disciplined minister will constantly
be seeking avenues to improve and further develop the gift
that God has granted. Again, much like physicians, it is cru-
cial to our assignment that we remain fresh and current with
the different theories and relevant issues that could help to
serve us in His cause. When ministry seminars are being
offered in communities (i.e., coping with clergy burnout,
dealing with the drug dilemma, avoiding and overcoming a
sexual indiscretion, etc.), it would be beneficial for most to
register or enroll in them to discover whatever tools these
courses may have to offer. This may be interpreted as an
overstatement of the point, but I am only trying to encourage
all associates to faithfully pursue education with diligence
and commitment.

The Ministry
of the Associate Minister

Associate ministers can be a real blessing to the ministry of a church. Their very presence in a church's ministry (particularly for those who were "birthed" into a church under the leadership of the current pastor) can generate a tremendous spark of spiritual energy in the life of that congregation. Such yieldings to the call of God all but guarantee the perpetuation of the proclamation of the Gospel for a people. It is a sure and encouraging sign of the effectiveness of the Word being declared among a people.

Who Am I?

It may seem that this is an absurd question for an associate minister to raise. On the other hand, a number of individuals who are "new" in ministry are facing a major identity crisis. Having been on the giving end of respect for pastors and other preachers, it is initially a bit strange and notably uncomfortable when one is on the receiving end of these same values. In view of this, it is no wonder that new ministers have difficulty with their sense of identity. "How should I now introduce myself?" "How should others refer to me?" "What is proper in accordance with ministerial ethics and etiquette?" These are some very real issues for many when first arriving in their new role in the community as a minister.

Traditionally (especially in our culture), preachers are referred to as "Reverend." The often used and quite acceptable alternative to this is the handle "Brother" or "Sister." Laypersons should always use a title when addressing ministers and should properly address them as either "Reverend,"

"Minister," or "Pastor," if such is the case. Whenever a minister is being introduced, or is just simply meeting new people, the same rule of courtesy should be politely applied. However, the minister him/herself should not as a general rule introduce themselves as "Reverend," particularly among other clergy. It is not known exactly why this is the case, but it is usually regarded as a gesture of arrogance and/or insecurity. Seasoned pastors could offer much assistance in this predicament by simply taking the initiative and making the introductions for their associates when in the presence of others who may not know them. Pastors should also publicly indicate to their congregations the appropriate method of addressing the new minister or associate, to establish immediately propriety on behalf of the new minister. There will always be a few peers of the neophyte who will contend that they should have special privileges. This miscalculation should be corrected early.

Native Born Ministers

Every local church can essentially be considered an incubator (a womb or nest) for ministry, a place where new servants (ministers) are "born," nurtured, and developed. These hallowed sanctuaries become then, the "operating room" where newborns are "delivered" and eventually launched into meaningful service for the Lord. The newborn associate should have a good working relationship with the pastor, and should be in regular company and communication with their "mentor" as they begin this new walk as a Christian minister.

The infant days for an associate are as critical as they are for the new baby in a home. These delicate times should be filled with meaningful sessions with one's pastor to learn as much as one possibly can upon assuming this assignment. When Paul met the Lord on the Damacus Road, he was immediately sent to the home of a seasoned saint named Ananias who laid his hands on him and tutored him for some time (see Acts 9:17-22). Even after this experience, Paul needed the credibility of a respected believer (and minister) named Barnabas to speak up for him and to confirm his calling before the disciples in Jerusalem. Consequently, one should not move too fast nor too far without the loving attention and blessed favor of the pastor of the church where you began your ministry. Associate ministers are much like college freshmen who desperately need orientation if they are going to effectively integrate the ranks of their new colleagues. To assume that one already knows is a dangerous attitude to have. Even the associate who is the biological offspring of the pastor should not make this presupposition. One must be careful to arrive at the occasion of their first charge (as an associate to a pastor) in a teachable mode, eager and willing to learn no matter what one already knows. The attitude of the boy Samuel demonstrates for each of us the proper perspective to maintain while learning the ropes of ministry. Eli the priest simply instructed him to say to the Lord, "...Speak Lord; for thy servant heareth..." 1 Samuel 3:9). Help us all to hear, Lord!

Migrants

Not all associate ministers, however, are born into the church wherein they hold membership. Sometimes they "migrate" into a pastor's life and work, possibly having come to the occasion already licensed, ordained, and even some with previous pastoral experience. Pastors may occasionally extend an invitation for one to come and join the ministry staff to help share the workload inherent to their assignment. At other times, they might be transferred to another city due to their primary job in a secular vocation, and subsequently (and quite appropriately) become part of a congregation in the town where they now reside. Still at other instances associate ministers join other churches as a result of their having become unfortunately dissatisfied or disgruntled or even unfulfilled with the pastor or the people in the church where they formerly attended. Whatever the case may be, it can still be a significant blessing to both the pastor, the people, and the associate if a thorough understanding is gained by everyone involved regarding the new opportunity before them to share in ministry in the same place.

Soon after arriving at another church, a previously licensed or ordained minister of the Gospel should immediately schedule a conference with the pastor to be formally introduced and to relate availability and interest in blessing the ministry of that pastor. It might be helpful to bring along a few basic things in this initial conference. They are the Certificate of License, Certificate of Ordination (if applicable), any other verifiable training certificates, and a letter of recommendation from their previous pastor indicating some kind of regard for the minister. Name-dropping and being overly familiar are practices that should be avoided at all times.

Whenever a minister arrives at the occasion of joining another church, it should be regarded that previous licenses and ordinations do not automatically qualify as grounds for acceptance and participation in the new ministry milieu. It is the sovereign responsibility of every individual pastor and church to endorse only those whom they feel exemplify those attributes needful for participation in the work of ministry under their authority. This is of particular importance when associates become involved with a ministry or a church, and transcend denominational lines to do so. Every denomination does not necessarily accept other denominations' credentials of a person's gifts. Each endorsing agency has its own set of guidelines and standards for certifying individuals for ministry. Associates should not become discouraged because of this, because any additional preparation can only help better qualify them for adequate service to His wonderful cause.

Respect

Interacting with the pastor can be a delicate endeavor. Whether publicly, privately, formally, or socially, associates should always be careful to hold the pastor in the highest esteem. Key in this aspect of their relationship is the matter of respect. Associate ministers must be careful never to cross the distinct lines that characterize the tenets of this relationship. The pastor is Pastor at all times. Whether at meat, over a cup of coffee, or during some recreational activity (i.e., basketball, golf, or shooting pool, etc.), pastors should be appropriately addressed as "Reverend" or "Pastor." No one (especially an associate minister) should ever take the liberty to address the pastor by using a first name or by saying "man" or "bud." This tragic mistake is made by many who want to be "buddies" with their pastor, particularly when the pastor is young or near the same age of the associate ministers. An old adage rightly states that "familiarity breeds contempt." The very nature of the office mandates the utmost respect. Even Paul was wise to suggest to his son Timothy, "Let no one despise your youth..." (1 Timothy 4:12). This viewpoint is for the young associate as well as older associates within the church. This is not about a person but rather a position. The pastor must be respected at all times, and elementary (in our culture) to this reality is to address them by an appropriate title.

Respect goes far beyond how one speaks of the pastor, but even how one addresses the pastor. It is quite phenomenal to see how some associates (and many church members) exchange and communicate with their pastor. The lines of demarcation that normally distinguish those relationships are obscured so often that they seem not to exist at all. Ours has become a culture of "contemptuous commoners." People have lost the sense of reverence for persons who serve in high offices, even with regard to the way the nation views the position of president of the United States. Thirty years ago, one would not dare hear of anyone referring to our nation's highest officer in the opprobrious fashion that persons do so today. The respectful regard for this position has literally been thrown out of the window. Even when news commentators make references to the President, they easily offer criticism without thinking about using the appropriate title "Mister." Things have sadly changed.

In spite of what may be the trend in politics and other arenas, there is a basic need for traditional values in this regard when it comes to referring to and addressing God's representatives (preachers and pastors). The associate should always be careful to extend every courtesy to the Lord's spokesperson in a church community. Tone of voice and language should ever reflect the highest good and the most sacred regard. God does not take it lightly when persons take it upon themselves to be disrespectful to His chosen vessels. He admonishes the world to "touch not mine anointed, and do my prophets no harm." (Psalm 105:15). When King Ahaziah had injured himself after falling through a lattice in his upper chamber (see 1 Kings 1:1-15), he sent messengers to inquire of a false god (Baalzebub) about whether he would recover. Elijah the Tishbite intercepted their journeying and told them to go back and tell him he was going to die. The king was so distraught with this unfavorable news, that he sent a captain along with fifty men to arrest Elijah and bring him to his office. When they arrived at the place where Elijah was sitting atop a hill, they disrespectfully demanded of him to come with them according to the king's orders. Elijah sarcastically refused and the Lord rained fire down upon them from the heavens for their rudeness. A second company of fifty and another captain were sent to forcibly (if need be) bring him to meet with King Ahaziah. Their approach was no less impolite, and the same thing happened; fire rained down from heaven and consumed them all. When finally the third posse was sent, this captain immediately came before Elijah and fell on his knees, and begged the prophet for mercy. The angel of the Lord told Elijah "...Go down with him: be not afraid..." (verse 15). The point of this illustration is quite clear. One must be careful when speaking to the servant of the Lord (or pastor). People simply cannot talk to God's anointed ones in any way they please. Even if the servant is wrong, one must never choose to become belligerent or contentious. Chastisement is a matter that God absolutely reserves the sovereign right and responsibility to impose Himself.

To underscore this further, when David and the entire host of Israel were returning the ark of the covenant to the city of Jerusalem, a related tragedy occurred. As they sang and paraded down the street towards the city, the ox that was carrying the ark stumbled along the way (see 2 Samuel 6: 5-7). Realizing that the ark may perhaps fall, Uzzah (one of David's nephews) reached up to grab hold of it to steady it before it fell. God was so incensed at him, that He immediately "...smote him there for his error..." (verse 7). The lesson here is unmistakable as well: God had spoken quite adamantly about touching the Holy thing (Leviticus 4:15), and Uzzah (even though he had the best of intentions) disobeyed God and paid the ultimate price for his misdeed. In effect God was saying (and is still saying today), "If I can't handle it, don't you bother it" (my interpretation).

One additional example sheds light on this very important fact. David was a fugitive in Israel, running for his life because of the jealous insecurity of King Saul. In 1 Samuel 26, David and Abishai (one of David's soldiers) found themselves having successfully breached the king's security and were literally standing over him while he slept in the bivouac site. Abishai requested of David permission to pin Saul to the ground with his spear. David's response is so revealing and quite right. He says, "...Do not destroy him; for who can stretch out his hand against the Lord's anointed,

and be guiltless?" (verse 9). What is so interesting about
this is that while Saul was indeed the Lord's anointed, David
was too (see 1 Samuel 16:13). Yet, David (God's chosen
successor to Saul) wisely recognized that he could not bother
the Lord's servant, even though Saul was clearly rebellious,
rejected, and a rascal. David understood that God reserves
the solemn right to chastise and discipline His own.

The whole point of these three Biblical stories is to
underscore the fact that pastors are to be respected at all
times, and especially by the associate minister at the church.
It is not the responsibility of human beings to frustrate the
ministry of leadership. People (but especially associates)
should exercise extreme caution in their interaction and involvement with God's leaders. He (God) hires them, and He
can fire them. Our best response in situations where things
have gotten clearly out of control, is to earnestly and fer-
vently pray. God can surely handle His business; we should
mind our own.

Attitude
This brings us to the matter of the associate minister's
attitude. The celebrated pastor, expositor, and writer Dr.
Charles R. Swindoll has defended a rather profound treatise
on the idea of attitude. He says:

> The longer I live, the more I realize the impact of attitude on
> life. Attitude, to me, is more important than facts. It is more
> important than the past, than education, than money, than
> circumstances, than failures, than successes, than what other
> people think or say or do. It is more important than appear-
> ance, giftedness, or skill. It will make or break a company...a
> church...a home. The remarkable thing is we have a choice
> every day regarding the attitude we will embrace for that
> day. We cannot change our past...we cannot change the
> fact that people will act in a certain way. We cannot change
> the inevitable. The only thing we can do is play on the one
> string we have, and that is our attitude...I am convinced that

life is 10% what happens to me and 90% how I react to it.

And so it is with you…we are in charge of our attitudes.

Indeed, attitude makes the difference. One must work diligently at all times to convey a spirit of humility and reverence. All ministers should understand that the call to ministry is a call to service. Servants function to meet a need at the will and pleasure of others (in our case, at the will and pleasure of God). All too often ministers of the Gospel assume that it is the responsibility of people to serve us (and there is a reciprocal relationship that exists between the pulpit and the pew). However, the service that ministers provide is not contingent on some earthly reward. The sincere minister knows that we are charged by God to go where He sends, say what He says, and do His bidding. Many times those assignments will not appear to have the desirable (mercenary) benefits one might prefer. That is why it is so important that ministers be good managers of their resources, and certainly not "…greedy of filthy lucre…" (1 Timothy 3:3). We are servants, willing workers in the Lord's vineyard. Our reward (and report card) is with the Lord in heaven.

We should be especially careful to always display a genuine heart for others and keep a servant's attitude. This should be the case in and out of the pulpit, and especially after one has preached. In fact, the part we play in the preaching ministry is largely incidental to what God is doing. As harsh as it may sound, God is really using us for His own purposes and good pleasure. We are really no more than faucets and hoses, conduits through which the water of His Word flows. With this in mind, Peter admonishes us that younger men should "be submissive to their elders" and always be "clothed with humility…" (1 Peter 5:5).

I recall that Rev. Nathan Dale, associate professor of homiletics at the School of Theology at Virginia Union University, told a story to our preaching class when I was pursuing my graduate degree. It seems that a young minister was scheduled to preach at his home church after having spent his first semester away in seminary. On the morning of his appointment, his grandmother called him to breakfast as per usual, but he declined, citing that he preferred to wait and not eat until worship was ended. His demeanor was markedly "vain" as he strutted around the house rather "peacock proud." Upon arriving at the church (intentionally late), he conspicuously strolled down the center aisle, nodding and gesturing subtly to his peers and loved ones, like a Hollywood celebrity at some awards show. With his head up in the air, he mounted the pulpit, shook hands with his pastor and proceeded to take his seat with an obvious air of distinction. When preaching time came, he made the normal scattered preliminary remarks, and commenced his pitifully pious presentation called the sermon. The people sat and did not move a muscle. One would have thought the young fellow was speaking Greek. Realizing that he had failed, when service was concluded, he shamefully came out of the pulpit with his shoulders down, his head bowed, his spirit rent, wishing that he didn't have to greet the people alongside the pastor at the front door as they exited. When at last he got home, he finally exploded. Blasting the parishioners, he exclaimed, "I don't understand those people. That was a good sermon. It was structurally sound and biblically accurate. I got an 'A' on that message when I prepared it for class." His dear old grandmother wisely spoke up and said to him tenderly, "Son, if you had simply gone up into the pulpit the way you did when you came down, you would have come down out of the pulpit, the way you did when you went up." I think this story makes my point.

Attitude extends far beyond the actual preaching event. How one regards oneself is very important in offering service to others. While God has so honored each of us to be involved in His redemptive work in community, we must be careful to consider our service with great meekness and modesty. We literally work for God to serve the needs of His people, and to be a blessing to them. When Paul was describing the symbol of sacrifice needful for "reasonable service" he ingeniously added that everyone should "… not think of himself more highly than he ought to think…" (Romans 12:3).

Before we conclude this discussion on humility, there needs to be a brief word said about listening to our friends, our family, and our fans. One of the most difficult lessons to learn for many an associate is the lesson on "how to receive compliments and criticism." Either of these "boulders" can be tremendous roadblocks on the freeway of successful ministry. Associates should learn not only to receive but even more so to welcome constructive criticism to improve their ministry. Real friends will readily be loving and honest and will tell you the truth, if one is willing to accept it. The best preachers in the world (of course, this is an arguable description) have close friends and associates with whom they have agreed to always be open and honest regarding various aspects of their ministries (particularly preaching). Constructive criticism challenges one's thinking and scholarship, and will surely make one a better student of the Word, and a better preacher of the Gospel.

Conversely, one should not take the exaggerated and overly generous reviews of booster clubs too seriously either. People, by nature, would prefer not to be honest if their candor will cause pain. For the most part, many will actually lie to avoid causing injury or hurt. Perhaps the best thing for many of us is to be told "the truth, the whole truth, and nothing but the truth." If we have "messed up," I surmise that it is only fair (to the minister, to the membership, and especially to the ministry) that someone lovingly and tenderly pull them aside and share with them the error of their way. Any self-respecting minister of the Lord will graciously receive the constructive criticism and take the necessary measures to correct the mistake.

Ethics

Morality and ethics are as critical and essential to effective Christian ministry as is clean air to the activity of breathing. All Christians should strive to conduct themselves in a fashion that clearly indicates their love and devotion to the Lord Jesus Christ. More especially, associate ministers (even pastors, for that matter) must be extra careful to "do the right thing" under any and all circumstances. A basic definition of ethics is simply decision making based on "what ought to be." It is quite different from the matter of *values*. Values are decisions based on what is important to the individual. Ethics clearly establish propriety based on the unmitigated matter of righteousness.

Life is a cycle of ethical decisions. The evils of our day keep the debate of morality and equity ever before us. With the blatant rise of deviant lifestyles, homosexuality, same sex marriages, euthanasia, capital punishment, abortion, alcohol consumption, drug use, human cloning, etc., the moral and social questions inherent to each of these are not likely to cease any time soon. The associate minister must demonstrate a strict adherence to "right living"! It must be known that certain things are clearly and predictably the case for every man and woman of God. Ministers can hardly expect to be taken seriously if the very practices about which they are admonishing others, are sadly corrupting them (see 1 Corinthians 9:27). If you are going to "talk the talk" then you must be determined to "walk the walk"! While a very few of these items are repeatedly the subject of universal debate, there should be no question or doubt when it comes to issues to which the Bible has offered unambiguous instructions. Our Christian conversion certifies a commitment to living and being morally right in compliance with the Word of God.

This is not a suggestion to say that the associate (or any minister for that matter) must be perfect. However, one should strive to live according to the holy standard forged by Christ. While it is utterly impossible for one to live sinless, it should be that every child (and minister in particular) of God ought "sin less." There are no set rules or practices that govern a number of areas of life for the minister, yet one must determine to "Let not then your good be evil spoken of..." (Romans 14:16). Any number of invitations and opportunities will be extended to the young preacher to attend certain functions and to participate in different activities. Our primary Text (the Holy Bible) does not address itself to many of them. The associate minister must be forced to draw his or her own conclusions and make those difficult decisions without the benefit of some written rule of practice. Under these circumstances, associates must be wise and careful to remember the sacred calling that empowers us, and determine to do nothing that would compromise their effectiveness or weaken their witness. Paul also added in verse 5 of Romans 14 that "...every man *(or woman)* be fully persuaded in his own mind" (parentheses mine). Whatever is done, one must remember that we work for God, who sits high and looks low. He sees everything and is taking copious notes.

Integrity

One might perceive that there is really no need to offer a discussion on the matter of integrity, especially for persons who have openly surrendered to the call of God in their lives. Quite on the contrary, the blatant lack of integrity among clergy has essentially weakened the witness of the church and all but rendered ineffective the work of many ministers who would dare to speak His name. If there was ever a need for a people of integrity, the time is now. My own personal definition for integrity is simply "saying what you mean, meaning what you say, and doing what you say and mean." This fundamental virtue is nothing but a by-product of character (fixed, predictable behavior). Associate ministers must be committed to these fundamental values in that a great number of others' decisions and beliefs will be significantly influenced by the words we say and the things we do.

When the late celebrated ABC news anchor Max Robinson was in his declining days, he continued to enjoy a periodic forum on the public speaking circuit. His untimely death was accented by an admitted life of licentiousness and promiscuity. It was during one such engagement at Howard University that he addressed himself to this matter of integrity before the student body of that historic black institution. What he said was so profound that, when the networks were documenting a few of his signal moments immediately following his demise, they revisited his presentation at Howard and broadcast him saying, "Whatever else you do in life, maintain your integrity. Regretfully, I lost mine. Please, don't you do that." After a significant pause he concluded, "After all, your integrity is really all that you have." In plain talk, he simply said, "your word is your bond."

People invest in what ministers say. Our words and our witness impact lives. One must settle the integrity issue from the outset. The kingdom does not need anything more to discourage men and women from choosing Christ as their portion. Our credibility must be incontestable. It should be noted that there is a distinct difference between credentials and credibility. Credentials are those items of endorsement that certify one's abilities based upon education, training, or some other demonstration of proficiency. Credibility, on the other hand, is the expressed confidence or trust in someone based upon their having demonstrated the ability to be reliable and honest. Credibility should never simply be understood (a given), it must always be established. The ministry needs more than ever men and women of integrity and honor to stand firm and speak with conviction about the ills of our society, and a God who can cure them all.

Accountability

If there is a single item that can jeopardize the existence of a healthy relationship between a pastor and any associate, I maintain that it is the issue of accountability. Associate ministers should recognize that as ministerial partners to a pastor, their service mandates a strict sense of duty to the idea of accountability. This arrangement should be considered a mentoring relationship, one in which the associate feels obliged to be answerable to the pastor. Of course, all of us are accountable to God; however, one must also give reverence and respect to the scriptural authority of the pastor. God has historically revealed His vision for a particular people to and through His chosen vessel – the pastor. One cannot realistically expect to become a good leader if one is not willing to be a good follower. It is in this "followship" role where the associate ministers learn their most valuable lessons outside of the active pastorate.

Associates should deliberately indicate to the pastor their whereabouts when not present for worship or other activities where their presence is expected. They should especially determine to be on time for the same. It should never be that an associate would enter the pulpit after the worship has begun, unless summoned by the pastor. Industry requires a strict adherence to time consciousness and attendance. The servants of the Most High should not present to Him anything less.

When given a task to perform, there should be no deviation from the expectation. There may be some that will offer uninvited commentary about how the assignment should be carried out, but associates must be careful to realize that they are being held accountable by the pastor. While we certainly want to please the Lord with the service that we may render, the pastor is the instrument of God to whom we must respond for direction and correction. Once the assignment has either been completed, abandoned or even inhibited, the

designated associate should report to the pastor any progress
or problems encountered during the execution of the same.
Accountability is a must and is highly important.

Authority

Every associate minister needs a forum wherein he or
she can be nurtured and possibly offered the marvelous privilege and opportunity to share in a church's vision for ministry, as the pastor may direct. Whether the associate is formally
trained or otherwise, ministry opportunities and compensa-
tion for the service are generally offered at the pastor's dis-
cretion, if the resources are available.

It should be firmly understood, however, that associate
ministers are not associate pastors or assistant pastors. They
are ministers who affiliate (or associate) with a particular
church's ministry, and are generally considered members
(upon making normal application and usually successful
completion of any New Member Orientation curriculum offered by the church), with all of the rights, privileges, and
responsibilities of other members. In that they are clearly a
special classification of member, they are accountable directly to the pastor (senior minister) and normally receive
all assignments, directions, and opportunities for service and
ministerial guidance from the pastor. They should never ar-
rogate unto themselves any authority or audacity for leading, directing, teaching, assigning, creating, initiating,
assuming, inviting, committing, obligating, manipulating, or
alienating any person(s), group, ministry fellowship, or part
thereof within the church without the specific direction and
blessing of the pastor.

Loyalty

Church ministry sometimes can become a contentious
environment. Strong opinions cause tension and passionate
discussions often ensue during business meetings and other
activities. What should be the associate's posture when this

occurs? Should they pose questions that challenge the leadership and vision of the pastor? Can they offer recommendations or make other verbal contributions to the discussions on these pertinent matters? Most pastors generally agree that associate ministers should exercise extreme caution in these deliberations. Let it be understood that associates are afforded the same rights, privileges, and responsibilities as other members. However, as has been previously asserted, they are a special (different) classification of member, because they (like the pastor) maintain that God has also spoken to and called them into this very important work. The reality is, though, that God assigns pastors (see Jeremiah 3:15) who in turn give oversight and leadership to the ministry of churches. Associates must be careful never to challenge the pastor's vision, authority, leadership, or decision making, especially not publicly. Nowhere in the Bible has God ever sought the approval or endorsement of an associate minister whenever He has spoken to His chosen servants. Whether one agrees with it or not, understands it or not, or likes it or not, the wise associate will always be mindful to support the leadership decisions of the pastor, particularly when the church is gathered and deliberating her business. If any associate minister has such urgent concerns that need to be addressed, then one should choose an alternate private forum to confer with the pastor on these critical matters.

At times, associate ministers have tragically found themselves caught up in the midst of a power struggle between the pastor and church. Unfortunately, they become manipulated by chronic complainers and begin to believe that they could do a better job than the pastor could. The wise associate minister will avoid entertaining any negative commentary from any member concerning the person or the position of the pastor. A quick admonition to encourage prayer and discourage further discussions is appropriate at all times. Otherwise, leave the politics alone.

Care should be given to ensure that the members of the church are not able to discern any semblance of disloyalty or dissension within the ranks of the ministers in the church. There will always be some in every church that will covet any occasion to frustrate the work of a pastor by stirring up controversy and dissension. Paul admonished believers in Ephesus to "Neither give place to the devil" (Ephesians 4:27). Associates should view the work of the pastor much like the role of the head coach. There cannot be but one head coach on the team at a time. If the team is to succeed, then the supplementary "coaching staff" must be on one accord and in sync with the head coach, or in this case, the pastor.

Obedience

One of the very first lessons I learned as a commissioned officer in the United States Army was the importance of simply knowing how to follow orders. This basic training reality is essential for the execution of successful maneuvers and the continued survival of the entire command. Likewise, if the local church is to enjoy effective service and maintain an atmosphere of divine order and spiritual control, the associate minister must learn the value of following the pastor's directives. Too many associates assume liberties (when given opportunities) that are outside the bounds of their instructions. One example of this is when asked simply to read the Scriptures, one makes the common mistake to either sing, give commentary, or even deliver a "mini-sermon" to the congregation first. Samuel's reverent admonition to Saul put it best when the king had stepped across the line of his specific area of assignment. The prophet said to him "...to obey is better than sacrifice..." (1 Samuel 15:22). Associate ministers should endeavor to do exactly what they have been asked to do. Honoring such privileges will surely help to create a strong relationship with one's pastor, gain the admiration and respect of the people, and also encourage the likelihood of future opportunities to serve.

Cooperative obedience does not insinuate that one is inferior or lacks courage. On the contrary, it is a sure sign that the associate is sensitive to the wishes and expectations of the pastor, and is further committed to honoring the task at hand by doing exactly what has been asked. Impromptu admonitions and unsolicited administrative directives to the church should always be avoided. The Holy Spirit does not tell any associate to say anything to a congregation that He will not reveal (or confirm) to the pastor.

Discipline

No thriving society can continue to enjoy success where there is no high regard for discipline. The good health and effective work of ministry in a church is not exempt from this reality. Sad to say, though, at regretful times, associate ministers have to be corrected and chastised when they have erred, whether the misdeed was intentional or unintentional. It is a necessary evil in the interest of preserving a wholesome Christian environment, and also purging "...out the old leaven" (1 Corinthians 5:7).

The acid test of real commitment for an associate minister is when during such correction or reproof by the pastor, one remains respectful and receptive to whatever disciplinary measures the pastor may feel led to impose to exhort the errant minister. Sometimes the result is silencing. This is when the pastor decides to withhold preaching privileges for a minister for some determined period of time. Other times, the transgressing associate may be required to make a public apology (depending on the nature of the offense), or be denied access to the pulpit (or other participation) until further notice from the pastor. Even at other times a pastor may choose to dock the associate's pay (if the associate is a member of the compensated staff) to underscore the seriousness of the indiscretion. An accompanying letter

of reprimand or memorandum for record may be drafted to
accentuate the specifics of the charges or concerns, and also
to minimize the potential of any misrepresentations which
might result because of the actions taken.

In whatever way it manifests, it is the responsibility of
the associate to cooperatively submit to the God-given authority of the pastor, and prayerfully endure the season of
suspension with humility and remorse. Whether the pastor's
actions are perceived right or wrong, it is the associate's
moral obligation to make sure that one's "...good is not
evil spoken of" (Romans 14:16). The church needs to
clearly recognize that the minister respects pastoral authority. Hebrews 13:17 firmly states that we are to "obey them
that have the rule over you, and submit yourselves: for they
watch for your souls, as they that must give account, that
they may do it with joy, and not with grief: for that is unprof-
itable for you." Pastoral directives to associates are generally given for devotion and not for motion (that is, vote or
formal deliberation). As the sports conglomerate Nike puts
it quite frankly, "just do it."

It is also important for the associate to observe the duty
to penitence and confidentiality during such reproof. It is
not the entire church's right to know the specific details of
these private dealings. It is further not the responsibility
(nor the right) of the associate minister to apprise them.
Care should be taken to ensure that one does not become a
busybody in these delicate undertakings, and inappropriately
begin to sow discord among the membership when chastisement or reprimand has transpired.

Temptation

Whether one likes it or not, it cannot be denied that
ministry is full of varying lures and temptations. It would
seem that the power to preach and do ministry should simultaneously be a divine "anesthetic" to the many enducements

of life. Unfortunately, such is not the case. The public acclaim associated with being in ministry is unquestionably both a blessing as well as a curse. On the one hand, the public limelight affords us the privilege of exposure to reach the most people we can to further perpetuate the message of the Gospel. On the other hand, it automatically ushers ministers into a highly visible arena that makes them the victims of continual demonic attacks. These range from the love of money, sexual licentiousness (and other immoralities), the egotism of leadership and power, to simply just being a user and a hustler. Associate ministers must be extremely careful to exercise every precaution to avoid these deadly traps that will surely weaken their witness, ruin their reputation, and cripple the ministry.

Everyone ought to know their limitations and weaknesses. There is no need to pretend that some things "do not bother us." There are some things that are indigenous to our calling and inevitably bother "all of us"! The sooner we can be honest with ourselves and become open to the help of others in overcoming those areas, the sooner we can be on the road to recovery and useful service to the Lord. Many persons choose to be in denial about their "problem areas" and prefer to avoid dealing with them altogether. At other times, some feel they can handle it alone and often find themselves failing miserably. My dad shared a story when I was growing up about a little boy whose mom had told him that he could no longer have any chocolate chip cookies. He obviously loved chocolate chip cookies and would often sneak and get one or two near mealtimes, which would subsequently spoil his appetite. One day the mother was passing through the kitchen and saw her little boy standing over the counter in a high chair with the lid off the cookie jar, staring down in a batch of freshly baked chocolate chips. She immediately yelled at the youngster, saying to him, "boy, didn't I tell you not to bother those cookies?" Startled, the boy replied, "But mom, I'm not bothering the cookies." She came closer to him and asked, "If you're not bothering the cookies, son, then what in the world are you doing?" He innocently said to her, "Mom, I just trying to learn how to resist temptation" (the topic of the Sunday school lesson he had studied at church). The mother slowly lifted the little lad off the high chair and pushed it away from the counter. She then replaced the lid on the cookie jar and shoved it back into the corner, and sat down at the kitchen table with her child on her knee. She then said to her boy, "Son, over the cookie jar, in a high chair, with the lid off, looking down at the cookies, is the wrong place to be when you're trying to resist temptation, especially when you like cookies." We might as well face it, it is utterly foolish to allow some situations to develop where the likelihood of falling or failing is great. The late Dr. Robert Dickerson of the Saint Paul Baptist Church in Pine Bluff, Arkansas, would frequently say to young ministers, "When God called you, He didn't dehumanize you." Know your limitations; be wise; and make it your personal commitment to even avoid the "...appearance of evil." (1 Thessalonians 5:22). No one has to spoon-feed a spirit-led person about how to stay out of compromising situations. Solomon put it plainly when he said, "...fear the Lord and shun evil." (Proverbs 3:7, NIV).

The best known exercise that is certain to encourage associate ministers in their escape from these dangerous situations is the activity of prayer. Jesus told His disciples that "...men ought always to pray, and not to faint." (Luke 18:1). Prayer (in my estimation) is the most effective tool we have at our disposal as ministers of the Lord Jesus Christ. It is essential if we are to avoid inappropriate settings and realistically resist temptation. The Reverend Curtis Brown of the Ebenezer Baptist Church in Sandusky, Ohio, said to me on the occasion of my installation celebration in Omaha, Nebraska, "If you keep your knees dirty, God will keep your heart clean." This profound statement should be stenciled on the hearts of believers everywhere, and absolutely every preacher of the Gospel. Pray! Pray! Pray!

Aspiration

There is nothing wrong with wanting an opportunity to preach, or even desiring to become a pastor. Paul wrote, "...If a man desires the office of a bishop, he desires a good work"(1 Timothy 3:1). However, such ambition and desire must be tempered so that it does not get in the way of cooperative service. Many associates become quickly obsessed with "getting a church" and resort to some rather loathsome tactics to facilitate the same. Parish ministry is not the only viable area of recognized Christian service. One does not necessarily need a pulpit in order to preach. Associate ministers should be careful not to actively court vacant churches nor compromise their dignity by making ridiculous concessions just for the sake of getting a hearing or securing a call. Our best service should be offered without regard for any earthen reward (even a church), and such that the Lord will be pleased with our offerings and assign us according to His will.

All of us should seek to faithfully serve His great cause in any capacity offered. There are certainly more opportunities to work in the life of a church than to preach. And since most churches only have one pastor at a time, it would be good to seek the pastor's advice about other ways to legitimately partner with that pastor's leadership.

Teaching a Sunday school class is an excellent opportunity to cultivate one's speaking and preaching gifts. Organizing a prison and jail ministry could offer tremendous challenges and provide marvelous forums for an associate minister to hone his or her skills. Visiting hospitals, ministering to senior's complexes, going to nursing homes and witnessing at local missions are a few examples of much needed areas of service where few give their time. The best thing to do is simply render oneself both willing and available to do whatever needs to be done when the honor to serve is offered.

Availability

Associate ministers must always be model Christians before, inside, and outside of the fellowship of the church. They should freely exhibit an eager interest and sincere willingness to serve and be used in any area of ministry service. In doing such, it reveals the selfless interest to encourage the pastor's assignment in light of the weighty burden that the pastor is charged to carry. Associates should readily avail themselves to share particularly in the following areas of ministry whenever called upon to do so:

1. In the administering of the ordained functions of baptism and communion and other assignments as determined by the pastor.
2. In the leading of worship through the reading of Scriptures, offering of prayers, leading in the shared reading of litanies, covenants, and other worship recitations.
3. In the preaching or teaching ministry of the church, should the pastor extend the opportunity to do so (even at a moment's notice).

(NOTE: All ministers should understand that preaching opportunities are not for the primary purpose for monetary gain and that often no honorarium may be given [see 1 Corinthians 9:16-18]).

The preaching ministry affords one innumerable opportunities to participate in service. Sitting and looking like a pulpit ornament is not one of them. Being idle and resembling some ministerial memento undisturbed in a trophy case is not part of our calling either. Anyone assuming such a posture has no idea what church ministry and our charge is all about. Associate ministers must be team players. They should be loyal and loving, and eager to confirm their willingness to serve at all times. It is this type of devotion to the work of a pastor that touches not only the hearts of a people, but also the heart of God. In demonstrating such, God is likely to consider more favorably such persons for promotions or other areas of service to His kingdom. A good example of this is seen in the life of Joshua, who, when the Lord's servant Moses had died, was honored by God with the distinction of becoming the next leader of that massive congregation of people towards possessing the Promised Land. Had he not demonstrated a clear commitment to Moses' ministry (see Exodus 17 and Deuteronomy 34), no doubt he would not have likely been selected by God nor respected by the people.

Visiting Churches

The best advice for any non-pastor or associate when not engaged or invited to preach is simply to stay at one's home church. "Church hopping" sends the terrible signal that a person is unstable and spiritually immature. This work is a discipline. The word "discipline" is a variation of the word "disciple," which means "learner." Worshiping at home is like eating at home. Parents would become understandably upset if their children consistently ate at someone else's house, especially when a meal has been prepared for them at home. Associate ministers should remember that their pastor is keenly aware of their spiritual diet, and is (or at least should be) preparing "meals" specifically designed to help strengthen and nourish them to good spiritual health. The danger in visiting is that one cannot be certain what will be served at another's "table." If the food (the Word) is not properly prepared, then spiritual "food poisoning" is likely to occur. Should no food be given at all on that occasion, then spiritual malnutrition is the obvious end. To encourage the probability that a "meal" will be served that is more likely to meet one's needs, then it is always best to eat at the table where food is being prepared by a "chef" who is sensitive to your spiritual needs. Furthermore, it is just not a good idea to be roaming around a city (especially looking for a preaching opportunity) anyway. Proverbs 18:16 says plainly, "Your gift will make room for you...." It does not say that ministers should make room for their gifts.

Accepting Invitations

As a matter of courtesy and respect, associate ministers should never confirm their availability to preach a sermon without first asking their pastor. Yes, God calls each of us to preach, and most of us have avowed to go wherever He would send us. But one should commit to being courteous and give reverence to one's pastor. It could be that the pastor might have plans to use the associate in some capacity during worship at home.

Furthermore, controversial circumstances may currently exist at the other church, about which the associate may or may not be aware, and the pastor might wish to offer relevant and discreet counsel. These are just a couple of real reasons why one should kindly consult with the pastor when considering acceptance of an invitation or a preaching opportunity.

Sermon Development Suggestions

Definition of Terms

Central to this task of developing a sermon and making preparations for preaching is a basic understanding of the language associated with sermon development. The following definitions of terms is offered to assist in this undertaking:

1. SERMON—A biblically based communication (written or spoken) relating a spiritual truth designed to effect a behavioral change in lives of the recipients.

2. PREACHING—The actual art of orally presenting a sermon.

3. TEXT—That portion or passage of Scripture from which the basis for the sermon is derived; it is the pericope.

4. CONTEXT—The immediate environment within which a text exists. It encompasses the complete circumstances pursuant to the selected text.

5. SUBJECT—The central idea or theme that is to be discussed in the sermon.

6. TITLE—What the person "calls" the sermon (the topic or name of it)!

7. PROPOSITION—A condensed and more thorough way of expressing the subject of the message.

8. OBJECTIVE—The planned (and written) result one hopes to obtain by the message—the goal.

9. THESIS STATEMENT or SYNOPSIS—A brief (concise) summary, containing the verbal content of the sermon.

It is expressed in three segments: (a) the textual situation (or condition of existence), (b) the complication, and (c) the resolution. Each segment is summarized in a complete sentence. Until the thesis or synopsis is summarized, no basis for inclusions or exclusions can be derived.

Looking for a Sermon

Distinguished orator and pastor, the late Dr. Sandy F. Ray has been quoted as having said, "sermon preparation is like a coal miner toiling under a landslide." He lived life with such a dedication that at the conclusion of every Sunday's sermon, he would go home with a keen sense of urgency, knowing that he had to prepare for next Sunday. Sad to say, a number of ministers do not possess that type of commitment. Many wait until the weekend and cram themselves into their studies in hopes of producing what is commonly known as a "Saturday night special." What often results is a pitiable presentation that one could hardly classify as a sermon.

It is my contention that sermon ideas should not be sought, as one would look for a bargain in a department store. Sermon inspiration should come as a direct result of one's cultivating their relationship with Jesus Christ through consistent prayer, a regular devotional life, intense Bible study, and one's spiritual reflections (meditating) over the Word and life's experiences. As the preacher demonstrates a love for Christ and His word, the Lord will always speak to them the message that He has for them. Based upon what God has said to them, a sermon can flow from them, which may eventually be delivered to God's people.

Thus, we have arrived at the relevant focus or purpose of every sermon. It is a spiritually charged presentation of the Word of God, which is delivered (preached) specifically to minister to the contemporary needs of the people. It should accurately and appropriately address itself to "where the people are."

Ideas and Inspiration

Creative ideas for preaching are abundantly around us. Most of the time, the stimulus is and should be the Word of God. After all, the Holy Bible is the primary reference or text from which all true preaching emerges. At other times, one may find initial insights or preaching motivation through a personal experience, a story, current events, a television show, a commercial, a comment, nature, science, history, technology, a speech or sermon, etc. At all times, however, the preacher must be careful that the inspiration for the message reflects biblical truth and sound doctrine, and not just some good idea or philosophy in life. Otherwise, the presentation is nothing more than a motivational speech. Preaching is certainly more than that.

To pursue this notion of inspiration further, a word of caution needs to be said about what I call manufactured inspiration. This is when a catchy title or common phrase is the motivating energy behind the sermon's development. Real inspiration comes as one's heart is genuinely and compassionately moved by the needs of a community of people, and not just some cute expression or coined phrase that catches the people's ear or eye. Second Timothy 3:16 reminds us that the Word of God is divinely inspired, and is subsequently beneficial for every task associated with its sharing.

The Preaching Privilege

The opportunity to preach before a congregation should not be taken lightly. It is a sacred trust. First of all, God has entrusted to all preachers His most precious commodity, that which He regards "... above all His name"—His Word (Psalm 138:2). A pastor, subsequently then, entrusts his God-given (and church-called) responsibility into the hands of his associate minister whenever a preaching opportunity is extended. It should be regarded reverently and gratefully, and not irreverently, tritely, or sacrilegiously. The task of preaching is designed to evangelize, to educate or enlighten, and to edify or encourage individuals. No greater insult to God and His people, or disservice to the preaching assignment is done than when a minister forces some contemporary phrase or expression upon the sermon title. This type of clear disrespect undermines the seriousness for the task, and shows a shameful lack of appreciation for the privilege and responsibility of preaching. A good example of such is when one minister took the passage in John 4 concerning Jesus' encounter with the woman at Jacob's well. After thoroughly reading his text, he gave for a title "He Met Her at the Well and Asked Her for Some." This is in my mind an abomination. The apparent inference in this expression is vulgar, to say the least. Another example is the common title of Tina Turner's hit song, "What's Love Got To Do With It," or the familiar best-selling novel and movie, *How Stella Got Her Groove Back*. In gist, the young minister should avoid these and other similar titles at all cost.

Choosing a Text

When considering a text, this pastor encourages young associate ministers to preach sermons about Jesus. All too often, eager and zealous young preachers have a tendency to want to correct, reprove, reprimand, and rebuke the congregation on issues of polity, practice, and procedure. This is a great danger that would do well to be avoided. It is not the responsibility of any associate to try and pastor the people in the sermon. The best way to avoid this tragic temptation is to focus your sermons around the birth, life, ministry, miracles, crucifixion, death, burial, resurrection, ascension, and imminent return of the Lord Jesus Christ. One can never have too many sermons about Jesus. The young minister should earnestly seek to communicate to the audience and pastor a genuine love and adoration for the Lord Jesus Christ. These type messages help to affirm their calling as they exercise their gifts for ministry before the people.

Preliminary Questions

Once a text has been selected, there are some basic issues that need to be established before the sermon is begun. The following questions are designed to help the preacher compile some essential tools before the actual sermon is constructed:

1. What is the basis of your inspiration for this sermon idea, or what is motivating you to develop this particular thought for preaching?

2. What is the main point of the text or passage to its immediate audience in its context? In other words, what was the apparent message for the people (or the individual) when the incident or expression in the text occurred? (NOTE: This information can be obtained through a thorough reading of the entire book, but especially the preceding chapters or passages which will allow you to put the passage into its proper context.)

3. What does the text say to you?

4. List some other significant issues in the text that obviously flow from the passage.

5. State the specific goal (in writing) that you are trying to accomplish by preaching this message. (Note: Goals must be behavior modification and results oriented and not cognitive, i.e., to show, to inform, to help them see, to make them realize, to get them to

understand, etc.). A behavioral goal is to cause your
listeners to do something (i.e., to surrender their lives
to Jesus Christ, to encourage tithing, to effect for-
giveness, to enlist volunteers for specific areas of
service, etc.).

6. Are there any key or difficult words (or phrases) that require additional research to help properly interpret the
passage?

7. What do other credible scholars and authors (commen-
taries, Bible study books, and word study texts) have to
say about the passage in question? This will provide
confirmation to your own scholarship and ability to
rightly interpret biblical passages. (NOTE: Be sure to
consult other's scholarship only after you have done
your own research and preparatory study, so that you
can learn to become your own commentary.)

When Does the Sermon Begin?

One might consider that the sermon starts when one has
stood behind the sacred desk and has begun to read the text.
Others suggest that the sermon begins the moment one en-
ters into the sanctuary and assumes a seat in the pulpit. In
actuality, the sermon begins long before that. My father
would always say, "I would rather see a sermon than to hear
one any day." In fact, the sermon is really an extension of
one's lifestyle and witness. How one conducts one's life
speaks volumes long before his or her voice is ever heard
bellowing through the speakers of a PA system. The
preacher must be careful to live his life consistent with the
message of the Gospel that we preach. Paul told the church
at Corinth that the Gospel he preached was certainly relevant and applicable to his own life. He made it clear that
he wanted to avoid the tragedy of having "... preached to others, and myself be disqualified for the prize" (1 Corinthians
9:29). He told the same fellowship that we are living

"... epistles, written in our hearts, known and read of all men" (2 Corinthians 3:2).

Since the sermon begins long before the sanctuary setting, then our disposition and deportment in the sanctuary is certainly important. The associate minister should be careful to sit with dignity and distinction. They should never sit slumped or slouched in their seats. Care should be given to ensure that their posture is fitting and proper, with both feet securely on the floor, and not bringing any unnecessary attention to themselves. Facial expression and uncontrolled eye movement hint unmistakably of the preacher's interests, and could render the sermon impotent even before it is preached. Talking, walking, picking with one's face or hair, all are cardinal no-nos. All incidental movement should be kept to a minimum, especially when one is seated before the congregation.

Types of Sermons

There are five basic classifications of sermons. They are expository, textual, topical, textual-topical, and narrative or story. What follows is a simple definition of each.

Expository sermons simply lay open the text, and allow the text to be the primary focus for the proclamation. It is literally taking a walk through the Word and letting the text do the talking. The word "exposition" perfectly describes the aim of this method of preaching—to expose. Its major points of emphasis are derived directly from the chosen text with the goal of explaining its truths and giving contemporary application for life's circumstances. Applying this approach is sure to make one a better preacher but will also help to create a mature Christian and church.

Textual sermons are also sermons that derive clearly from within the text. The preacher, however, builds the sermon from a word, a verse, several verses, or inherent issues that unfold from either the selected text or other supportive texts.

Topical sermons are sermons that are developed primarily based upon the title that the preacher chooses to call the message. They are usually biblically sound and accurate; however, its themes or major divisions are generally derived independently of the chosen text.

Textual-topical sermons are a creative combination of both the textual and topical methods.

Narrative or **Story** preaching is based upon a biblical story that is conveyed in the Scripture that has its own themes and segments. The details in the narrative lend to the sermon its shape, movement, and content, from which any relevant application can be derived.

It should be easy to deduce based upon the questions given earlier in this document that this pastor is a very strong advocate of young preachers' (in particular) developing a real commitment to the art of expository preaching. The purpose of this is to help make the task of preaching as unencumbered as possible; simply let the text speak. This minimizes the dread of coming up with things to say and offers the most credible information for sermon building that can be used in developing the message—the information in the text.

Structuring the Sermon

Now we devote our attention to the matter of organization and structure. There must be recognition that organization and structure are fundamental parts of the proclamation process. One must have a plan in the formulation of the ideas for the sermon. This aspect should not be viewed as a burdensome task, but rather regarded as an integral part of the entire work. In light of this, any structure should contain a minimum of an introduction, the body, and a conclusion. Let us consider a few points on each of these.

The Introduction

The introduction is the first critical part of the sermon. It should not be treated lightly. It can make or break the entire message. Effectively introducing a sermon is like a real estate agent showing a house. Before entering, the prospective tenants must come onto the porch. If the porch is not stable or presentable, then most potential buyers will not demonstrate much interest in purchasing the house. Likewise, the sermon must have an attractive "porch." The introduction, in effect, becomes the lure that captivates the attention of the listeners. It should create a high level of interest, be clear, logical and have continuity. Creativity is encouraged, but not at the expense of compromising the content of the message to follow.

The Body

Inside this segment of the sermon is contained what is known as the homiletical plot. Herein is the heart and soul of the message. The main body of the sermon should follow the plot form of a good story. The preacher should avoid every opportunity to upset its equilibrium, like "chasing rabbits." Such meandering can jeopardize the goal or objective, and cause the hearers to become distracted and jump the track at some point in the sermon. The Gospel content should plainly emerge in the body, so as to clearly offer the audience a solution to whatever dilemma with which they might be faced.

The Conclusion

No pilot graduates from the flight academy simply because he has mastered the art of take-off and can fly the plane. A successful trip includes not only the take-off but also the landing. Likewise, the effective proclaimer of the Gospel must order his sermon like a skilled navigator negotiating his way through an orienteering course. He must know exactly where he is going if he is to cause others to reach the same objective. In pursuit of such, the conclusion must be carefully planned just like the other parts of the sermon. It should be climactic and not anti-climactic. It should clearly resolve and bring obvious closure to the issues raised throughout the body of the sermon. Once the conclusion is revealed, the preacher should bring healthy closure to the entire presentation. He should never open any new issues at this point, because it would certainly frustrate the flow of the sermon and conceivably, the workings of the Holy Spirit in the hearts of the congregation.

Illustrations

The use of illustrative materials in the sermonic discourse can contribute greatly to the effects sought from the message. A good illustration in a sermon is like a window inside a house—it lets the light in. Their usage can help clarify otherwise obscure truths or ideals through imagery and word pictures. Used properly, an illustration can drive home a point that might otherwise be overlooked.

One must be careful not to overburden a sermon with too many or unnecessary illustrations. They ideally are designed to enhance and to be an attractive addition to the sermon, rather than to be a disastrous distraction in the sermon. While illustrations are supposed to attract and arouse attention, if misappropriated, they can arrest the audience's attention such that they might not hear another word the preacher is saying. If the sermonic point can be effectively made without an illustration, it might well be wise not to use one.

A word should be said about the source of illustrative materials. Sermon illustrations need not be entirely from some manual or text on illustrations. Everyday circumstances often lend to preaching the best examples to highlight the point being made in the message. Current events, child-rearing experiences, conversations, newspaper articles, animals, even nature can become a wonderful source to help make a point clear.

Preaching Methods

A final word should be offered beyond the matter of the message, to the issue of the method, that is, how the sermon is to be delivered. There are a number of contemporary examples that demonstrate legitimate approaches to the art of preaching. Having been a student of the craft for nearly all my life, I have drawn some conclusions about the practice that inform the positions which I now share. It appears that there are basically four styles of preachers.

First, there is the *manuscript* preacher. This describes one who arrives at the preaching moment with a full-length manual text (hopefully which the preacher has personally written) from which the sermon is presented. With rare exception, the manuscript preacher will not deviate from the written page that holds the content of the sermonic discourse. Nonetheless, this preaching method ensures a commitment to the information collated in preparation. It can be a quite effective delivery method, if the minister is securely acquainted with the script, and can master his manuscript in delivery, rather than be mastered by the manuscript.

Secondly, there is the *outline* preaching approach. The minister who employs this method will usually have a piece of paper or some note cards upon which the principle points or major themes are written. They usually appear secure and assured of the issues to be addressed in the meat of the message, but are peculiarly blessed to be able to convey it without a need for a complete manuscript in front of them. Done properly, this can also be quite an effective (even impressive) preaching method.

Thirdly, there is the *extemporaneous* preacher. This practitioner in ministry has also prepared a sermon (it may or may not be written) but comes to the occasion of the sermon without the benefit of a manual text or even notes. The preacher is generally well acquainted (and to some degree) confident with the information being delivered, such that there is little or no dependence on a paper or notes. This individual is usually an organized thinker and possesses a particular spiritual endowment for the effective proclamation of the Gospel via this method.

The fourth method that is manifesting on the preaching scene is what I call the neo *"memeo-script"* method. These highly skilled "ministerial machines" have thoroughly prepared a full-length manuscript. However, rather than bringing the actual script to the proclamation occasion, they have ingeniously committed every detail of their sermon to memory. It seems more of a mechanical sermon presentation, however quite effective (as far as their being able to efficiently and accurately impart their information is concerned). I caution the adoption of this method, because there is little opportunity for fresh inspiration from the Holy Spirit during the presentation. If one becomes a slave of their memorized message, then any deviation from the script would likely result in catastrophic circumstances. A popular minister who employs this preaching style was delivering one of his familiar sermons in a different city. However, some "fans" from a revival in one of his previous invitations drove to hear him. The disappointment was quite tragic because (according to them), they had purchased the tapes from their hometown revival where he had preached, and reported that it was just like listening to the tape, from his rhythm and cadence to every gesture and tonal inflection.

The Actual Preaching Event

Much could be said about the actual act of preaching in this manual. There are quite a number of books already written which give much attention to this issue. However, I would offer a few comments regarding the preaching event that I contend could be helpful to us who base our method of proclamation largely on the examples set before us.

Style

It must be understood that preaching is not a performance. It is a spiritual presentation under the influence of the Holy Spirit through which the preacher authentically puts together personal experience in light of the biblical tradition. The preacher is a live witness to the truth of the Word, and must be careful to share it truthfully. In other words, there is no place for cloning and mimicking in the preaching event. Genuine and authentic proclamation emerges from the very being of the preacher designed to share some aspect of the faith implicitly. No amount of energy and animation, theatrics or gyrations can substitute for honesty and integrity during the sermon. Such ministerial aerobics and acrobatics disgrace the sacred charge to which we have been called and dishonors the God we serve. Honesty enhances believability. Anything other than a credible presentation of the Gospel through the personality of the preacher dishonors and desecrates the sacredness of our charge.

Preachers should earnestly seek to convey authenticity and realness if they are to be convincing to their hearers. Each listener should reach the clear conclusion once the sermon is ended that "I believe him (or her)." The preacher must show integrity and virtue to his or her own personality. God has so created us that just like our fingerprints, we each have our own unique personality. We should work hard to genuinely be ourselves when preaching. Otherwise, our presentation becomes an awful form of entertainment, and the last thing any committed preacher of the Gospel should seek to do is to impress or amuse the pew before whom we declare God's Word.

Attire

In this same vein, the minister should arrive at the occasion of preaching properly attired in a conservative robe or dark suit (preferably black or blue), and a crisp white shirt. Women should use comparable modesty as well. Their dresses should be sufficiently lengthy (with no splits) and loose enough not to inordinately accentuate the body's form, and their blouses should not immoderately expose cleavage. It is simply phenomenal to witness the number of preachers (pastors and associates alike) who would dare approach the sacred task of preaching dressed in loud red, pink, yellow, or orange apparel. The appearance of the preacher should reflect as much concern for reverence and sincerity as the proclamation itself. One should be careful to minimize the use of flashy accessories. Our listeners could hardly take us seriously if when we showed up to preach, we arrived adorned in what appears to be a "Mr. T start-up kit." Excessive jewelry (i.e., extravagant rings on every finger, gaudy chains and wrist bracelets, or over-decorated robes, etc.) must be avoided emphatically. These can become significant deterrents to the effectiveness of our hallowed preachment.

Posture

Pulpit presence is as critical to the preaching event as is the proclamation itself. The incorporation of relevant movements and gestures during the sermon must be regarded very seriously. If not, bad habits are sure to overshadow the communication of truth and render dubious the message being shared. The minister should endeavor to stand erect with both feet firmly placed flat on the floor during the preaching event. Standing erect does not suggest that one must stand at "attention" (as if in the military). If one's knees are locked while presenting a sermon, eventually the poor circulation will result in the preacher becoming lightheaded and possibly fainting. The important thing is simply to stand properly (not slumped over or leaning on one leg), head up, shoulders back, and eyes focused ahead, to effectively engage the congregation during the presentation.

In addition to standing correctly, proper management of one's hands is vital as well. One of the worst habits ministers develop during preaching is what is commonly known as "counting change." It refers to the terrible practice of placing one's hand(s) inside the pocket and jingling the coins or picking with the lint inside during delivery. This seems to be a nervous reaction to try and help one settle with the idea of standing before a congregation in an attempt to get comfortable. It should be remembered, however, that one should never become comfortable handling the sacred treasures of God's Word. Preaching is an event that poises the minister precariously between two worlds—earth and heaven, between humanity and Divinity. One is literally speaking to sinful people on behalf of a Holy God. The last thing one should seek to do in this awesome assignment is to become "comfortable" or "at ease" in the presence of such Holiness. The proper thing to do is humbly place one's hands at one's sides (one hand may be modestly placed on the podium) and prayerfully proceed through the sermon.

Another practice that is also becoming more and more common among some ministers is the new custom of "mike-holding" and walking during the sermon. Some have adopted this method in an effort to promote a sense of security (confidence) with the message and to assert one's independence of a need for a manuscript. I contend some of this is based largely on the images of popular television preachers who are consistently seen vacillating across the pulpit stage like an ecclesiastical pendulum. The danger in this practice is clearly that the listeners' focus during the preaching is more likely to become drawn to the proclaimer rather than the proclamation. It is the firm position of this writer that the less conspicuous the preacher, the more effective the preachment.

Pace

The tendency for many a young minister at preaching time is to "hit-the-ground-rolling." Before you know it, the preacher is scurrying along at such a rate of speed that even before the sermon has sufficiently gotten off the "runway" the congregation is exhausted and trying to catch their breath, wondering if the minister is going to make it through or not. Some, on the other hand, lean toward an exaggerated slow rate (pretending to be old), such that it overburdens the sermon and the congregation. There is no need to become "old" before your season. Time and age will certainly slow one down soon enough. A sermon must have a comfortable rate. The best rule of thumb is simply to take your time and effectively manage the allotted time you have been given.

Duration

The attention span of people is increasingly becoming smaller. It has been suggested that we forget 50% of what we hear within the first 24 hours of a 20-minute presentation. Within 48 hours, we have forgotten 75% of what we have heard. After 72 hours, the average individual will remember only approximately 10 to 12% of what may have been given in a sermon or oral presentation. If this is true, then the matter of a sermon's length and time is critical in preaching.

It is not known exactly why, but worshipers are finicky listeners. They usually only want to hear the pastor. Periodically, they will graciously receive a gifted guest minister or perhaps another pastor who may visit. Most of the time, however, associate ministers are tolerated at best, especially for those who are new in ministry and have limited preaching experience. This is not to say that associates cannot preach. There are a number of talented and extremely gifted associate ministers staffed throughout this country. It seems the acceptable and commonly suggested duration of an associate minister's sermon should not exceed 25-30 minutes. A pastor may effectively get away with preaching for an hour, and the congregation would hardly wince or move. However, if an associate tried to get away with the same thing, he would be a long time getting another opportunity to preach before the church. The best advice is simply to stay within the allotted time. One cannot tell it all in one single sermon, anyway. There will likely be other opportunities extended to preach.

Voice

The voice is the most important tool we have at our disposal in the preaching ministry. It is the principle medium through which the message of the Gospel is delivered. Effective management of it is critical if our proclamation is to be reasonably received. While we have little to do with the type or quality of "tool" that we have been given by God, there are some practical helps and suggestions which might assist us as we use what we have.

Preaching is not a shouting contest. It is not an exercise in screaming and yelling. It is an oral communications activity expressed with passion and emotion. Its aim or goal is not to emotionalize or stir the people. They indeed might become emotional, but that should not happen as a result of the preacher's seeking to effect such. Whenever God's people are moved during a sermon, it should be only because of the power of the Word of God. A preacher's volume and tonal inflection are not considered measures of one's power. Effectively incorporating variety during the presentation can enhance the impact of the message, but the preacher should never seek to emotionalize the people through some skillful manipulation of his vocal chords. Preaching is a natural spiritual exercise under the influence and anointing of the Holy Spirit.

Readiness

Every associate minister should always be ready to preach. Most "old-school" pastors suggest that every preacher should always have at least two sermons with them at all times—one in the pocket, and the other one in the heart. This is excellent advice even for the seasoned pastor. I contend that a preacher who is not pastoring (and not preaching with a great degree of frequency) should constantly be working on a sermon. Some pastors require their associates to write a complete sermon for them each week. This may (or may not) be realistic, but the discipline inherent to this task is essential. If not a full-length manuscript, then associates should at least have a written sermon idea, an established goal, and a working outline reflecting the focus of their current inspiration. This type of training will be of much benefit to the preacher, and will encourage a practice that will lessen the likelihood of the last-minute study habits adopted by many.

Summary

Much more could be said to encourage the work of associate ministers. I have not even begun to scratch the surface of the many exhaustive subjects. The goal sought here was primarily to offer pragmatic helps that reflect the viewpoints of experienced pastors who have corporately tutored thousands of young ministers serving near their sides. Dialogue will hopefully ensue between pastors and preachers everywhere to facilitate relationships while serving God's people.

Every situation is different. These are not considered hard and fast rules. It is my prayer that these suggestions will ease the tension between pastors and associates, and enourage their relationship as servants of God. I also pray that every associate so called to be partners with a pastor in ministry would approach these weighty tasks with much seriousness, and trust God to breathe upon their efforts with His divine favor. I say again, that a call to preach is a call to preparation. Someone has aptly stated that to "plan to fail" is to "fail to plan." Let it never be said that any preacher of the Gospel who partners with us in this field of labor is guilty of arriving at the preaching moment having not adequately prepared to credibly represent our God.

With the varying needs of our congregations and the tremendous workload of the ministry of the pastor, the privilege to serve as an associate should not be regarded lightly. It is a serious charge. Providence has called us, pastors are depending on us, and the people are watching us.

Most professional athletes do not enter the league as starters. Many times they are constrained to assume a seat on the bench in a back-up role. No team can thrive and continue to survive without a healthy "bench" of players on the sideline, since starters cannot always stay in the game. Good alternates always keep their mind in the game, cheerfully offer support and encouragement, and continue to train and stay in condition, just in case their number is called. Considering the seriousness of it all, I encourage associates to humbly do the same thing. You never know, you might be next to come off the bench. I pray you are ready when called. Thank God for associate ministers!

Appendix

Some Do's And Don'ts for Associate Ministers

(The Twelve Commandments of the Associate Minister)

1. Pray without ceasing and always be ready. You never know when an opportunity will occur.
2. Never ask (or hint to) a pastor for the opportunity to preach.
3. Never enter the pulpit uninvited.
4. Do only (and exactly) what you have been asked to do — no more, no less.
5. Always be ready to assist your pastor and alert to respond to any spontaneous need.
6. Volunteer for service opportunities beyond preaching where obvious needs exist.
7. Always inform your pastor whenever you will be absent from church.
8. Never accept an invitation without first asking your pastor.
9. Never consent to do a wedding without your pastor's authorization.
10. Never counsel members without your pastor's permission.
11. Don't take too seriously the praise of your friends, your family, and your fans.
12. Always remember that *loyalty* paves the way to *opportunity*.

Suggested Questions for Ordination

When responding to the following questions and statements, the candidate should be able to offer biblical references to verify answers. These questions are worded such that they lend themselves to adoption by any denominational perspective. These questions may be expanded or elaborated on as the catechizer or council may see fit.

1. Describe your conversion experience.
2. What is salvation?
3. What is the Bible?
4. Who wrote the Bible?
5. Who is Jesus Christ?
6. Define the church.
7. What is the purpose of the church?
8. Describe your call into the Gospel ministry.
9. Define preaching.
10. What is the purpose for licensing?
11. What is the purpose for ordination?
12. What are the biblical officers of the church?
13. What are their qualifications for these areas of service?
14. Define pastor.
15. Define deacon or elder.
16. What are the principle doctrines that govern your denomination?
17. Name them.
    (Note: For Baptists, they are the Articles of Faith.)
18. How many books are there in the Bible?
19. What are the major divisions?
20. How many books are there in each division?
21. What are the biblical ordinances of the church?
22. Define each of those ordinances.
23. Distinguish between immersion and other methods of baptism, and defend your preference.
24. Define autonomy.

25. What is the difference between a theocracy and a democracy?
26. How does one become a member of a church?
27. How may one be dismissed from a church?
28. How is the church to obtain finances to accomplish its mission?
29. What are your views on theological education for ministers?
30. What is a denomination?
31. What is your denominational affiliation?
32. Why are you aligned with this affiliation?
33. Who is your pastor?
34. What is the name of your church wherein you currently hold membership?
35. What is the name of your District or Association?
36. Who is the Moderator or Presiding Minister?
37. What is the name of the national organization with which you are affiliated?
38. Who is your national president or presiding minister?
39. Who is the mayor of your city?
40. Who is the governor of your state?
41. Who is the president of the United States of America?
42. What is your position on marriage?
43. What is your position on co-habitation?
44. What is your position on divorce?
45. What is your position on abortion?
46. What is your position on homosexuality?
47. What is your position on same sex marriages?
48. What is your position on gay rights and civil government?
49. What is your position on drug use?
50. What is your position on alcohol consumption?
51. What is your position on capitol punishment?
52. What is your position on suicide?
53. What is your position on assisted suicide?

54. What is your position on paralegal gambling?
55. What are your views on resolving conflict in the church?
56. What is your position on women in ministry?
57. What is your position on teenage or unmarried pregnancy?
58. What is your position on baby dedications for babies conceived out of wedlock?
59. What is your position on funerals for the unsaved and the unchurched?
60. What should be your relationship with the pastor?
61. What is your position on counseling?
62. What is your position on counseling the opposite sex?
63. What should be the minister's relationship to family?
64. What should be the minister's involvement in government and politics?
65. What should be the minister's response to social invitations?

SERMON EVALUATION

Preacher's Name _____   Date: _____

Text: _____   Title: _____

I. PRESENCE:					
a. Neat and well groomed.	1	2	3	4	5
b. Attire (accessories).	1	2	3	4	5
c. Posture.	1	2	3	4	5
d. Eye Contact.	1	2	3	4	5
e. Gestures.	1	2	3	4	5
f. Confidence.	1	2	3	4	5
g. Sincerity.	1	2	3	4	5

II. PREPARATION:					
a. Biblical and Theological Soundness.	1	2	3	4	5
b. Use of Illustrative materials.	1	2	3	4	5
c. Familiarity with manuscript or message.	1	2	3	4	5
d. Text - Title compatibility.	1	2	3	4	5
e. Clearly outlined structure.	1	2	3	4	5
f. Stated goals and objectives.	1	2	3	4	5
g. Introduction and conclusion.	1	2	3	4	5

III. PROCLAMATION:					
a. Vocal control (naturalness).	1	2	3	4	5
b. Comfortable rate or pace.	1	2	3	4	5
c. Pronunciation.	1	2	3	4	5
d. Energy (animation).	1	2	3	4	5
e. Passion and sincerity.	1	2	3	4	5
f. Believability.	1	2	3	4	5
g. Language (imagery).	1	2	3	4	5
h. Clear central idea.	1	2	3	4	5
i. Development or major themes.	1	2	3	4	5
j. Engagement of listeners.	1	2	3	4	5

IV. COMMENTS: (May comment on congregational analysis)

_____
_____
_____
_____
_____

RATING SCALE
  1 - Excellent   3 - Average   5 - Needs Improvement
  2 - Above Average   4 - Below Average

Signatures below indicate that the preacher and Pastor have met to discuss this review.

Signature: _____   Pastor: _____

Date: _____   Date: _____

Use a separate sheet of paper if additional space is needed for comments, goals, or substantiation.

Terryfic Concepts, Inc.®

MINISTER PERFORMANCE EVALUATION

Name: _____ Evaluation Period: _____

Position: _____ Evaluator: _____

I. ATTITUDE:					
a. Demonstrates a commitment to ministry.	1	2	3	4	5
b. Eager towards tasks.	1	2	3	4	5
c. Accepts criticism and suggestions.	1	2	3	4	5
d. Performs under stress.	1	2	3	4	5
e. Is a "team player."	1	2	3	4	5
f. Respects leadership.	1	2	3	4	5

II. LEADERSHIP:					
a. Establishes realistic personal goals.	1	2	3	4	5
b. Works to accomplish church's vision.	1	2	3	4	5
c. Works to accomplish church's mission.	1	2	3	4	5
d. Organizes and prioritizes tasks.	1	2	3	4	5
e. Cooperates with other leaders/staff.	1	2	3	4	5
f. Sets and enforces high standards.	1	2	3	4	5
g. Delegates responsibility.	1	2	3	4	5
h. Motivates and encourages others.	1	2	3	4	5
i. Offers guidance and assistance.	1	2	3	4	5
j. Able to resolve problems/difficulties.	1	2	3	4	5
k. Follows up tasks assigned.	1	2	3	4	5
l. Seeks self-improvement.	1	2	3	4	5
m. Respected by others.	1	2	3	4	5

III. PREACHING AND TEACHING:					
a. Prepared for the occasion.	1	2	3	4	5
b. Written communication skills.	1	2	3	4	5
c. Oral communication skills.	1	2	3	4	5
d. Authentic and natural in delivery.	1	2	3	4	5
e. Engages listeners.	1	2	3	4	5
f. Relevance of sermons/ materials.	1	2	3	4	5

IV. PASTORAL CARE:					
a. Passion for souls.	1	2	3	4	5
b. Availability.	1	2	3	4	5
c. Sick visitation ministry.	1	2	3	4	5
d. Sensitivity to others.	1	2	3	4	5
e. Patience and tolerance.	1	2	3	4	5
f. Listening skills.	1	2	3	4	5
g. Regard for confidentiality.	1	2	3	4	5

RATING SCALE

1 - Excellent	3 - Average	5 - Needs Improvement
2 - Above Average	4 - Below Average	

Signatures below indicate that the preacher and Pastor have met to discuss this review.

Signature: _____ Pastor: _____

Date: _____ Date: _____

Use a separate sheet of paper if additional space is needed for comments, goals, or substantiation.

Terryfic Concepts, Inc.®

Suggested Reading

Craddock, Fred B., *Preaching*. Nashville: Abingdon, 1985.

Crum, Milton Jr., *Manual on Preaching*. Valley Forge: Judson, 1977.

Forbes, James A. Jr., *The Holy Spirit & Preaching*. Nashville: Abingdon, 1989.

Mitchell, Henry H., *Celebration & Experience in Preaching*. Nashville: Abingdon, 1990.

Moebuhr, H. Richard, *The Purpose of the Church and Its Ministry*. New York: Harper & Row, 1956.

Nance, Terry, *God's Armor Bearer-How to Serve God's Leaders*. Tulsa: Harrison House, 1990.

Nance, Terry, *God's Armor Bearer-Book II*. Tulsa: Harrison House, 1994.

Spurgeon, Charles H., *Lectures to My Students*. Grand Rapids: Zondervan, 1954.

Vines, Jerry, *A Guide to Effective Sermon Delivery*. Chicago: Moody, 1986.

Wardlaw, Von M, *Preaching Biblically*. Philadelphia: Westminster, 1983.